GW00320441

Book 1
Genesis

In the Beginning

Written by Anne de Graaf

Illustrated by José Pérez Montero

Adventure Story Bible

Bible Society

Genesis — In the Beginning

Contents — Genesis 1-22

Old Testament Introduction

God has loved people ever since he made the first person, many, many years ago. The Old Testament tells story after story of the ways in which God has taken care of men and women through the years. Again and again he gave people the choice between doing good and bad.

Although he punished those who disobeyed, it was because he wanted people to become all they were meant to be, because he wants what is best. The Old Testament tells the story of God's people, the descendants of Abraham.

God called one man to follow him, and that man, Abraham, listened for the voice of God. Because Abraham believed in God and trusted him, people learned who the one, living God is. The Lord made promises to Abraham and kept them.

Many years later, when God gave Moses the ten commandments, God's people had a Law which they could follow. They had a measuring stick by which to tell right from wrong. Yet again and again people chose to do wrong, and as the years went by, God's people went from war to war, and from bad to worse.

There were people who listened to God and tried to remind God's people to keep his Law. These were the prophets. They helped make God's people faithful to him, and told the kings God's word.

In the Old Testament you can read about all that happened between God and his people, before Jesus came to live in the world.

Book 1 — Bible Background

The Book of Genesis is a book of beginnings. It begins the Bible. It describes the beginning of the world — how God made the first people, the first animals, and all the earth. It contains very old stories which tell about people who began to act in bad ways and hurt each other, about a terrible flood that swept everything away, and about a very important man called Abraham.

Abraham was another beginning. He was the father of God's chosen people. Genesis tells about Abraham, his son, his grandchildren and his great-grandchildren.

If you were to put your hand in the soil and trace round your fingers, you would see a picture of your hand. You made that picture. But did you ever wonder who made your hand? Where did you come from?

You came from your mother and father. And they came from their parents, on and on down through the generations. If you go back far enough, you will come to the first man and woman who ever lived on earth. But where did they come from? What happened in the beginning?

WHO MADE THE WORLD?

God Makes Everything

Genesis 1.1–19

A long time ago there was nothing but darkness. It's hard to picture just nothing, but that is all there was, except for God.

So God made light, and that way there could be day and night, instead of only darkness.

Then God made the sky and the earth and divided parts of the earth into oceans and seas, and other parts into big pieces of land. God made all the plants and trees and made them grow on the land.

God reached into the sky and made the stars and planets. He made the sun and moon so there would always be a day after every night, and spring after every winter.

God made these things, just as you can make a picture of your hand in the soil.

When he saw all the beautiful waterfalls and mountains, roaring waves and bright blue skies, he knew there was still more to make.

It Looks Good

Genesis 1.20–25; 2.1–6

God looked at all the water covering the world, and decided to make animals to live in the seas. He made big fish and little fish, and many underwater plants. Some were too small to see, while others reached from the bottom of the sea all the way to the surface.

For the sky he made big birds and little birds — bright blue, dark green, and many other colours.

When he looked towards the land, God saw grass blowing in the breezes and ripe fruit hanging from the trees. He knew it was a good place for animals so he made tiny bees and giant elephants, crocodiles, sheep, lions, and all different sorts of animals, but they did not have names yet. There was plenty of food and water for them all.

When God stopped creating the animals, trees, birds, and fish, he looked at all he had made. He was very pleased. Yet he knew there was still more to make.

The First Man and Woman

Genesis 1.26-31; 2.4-7, 18-23

At that time there were no people on the earth. God wanted to make someone who would be like him, just as you are probably like your mother or father. So he made the first person.

He took a handful of dust, blew on it, then created a life that was the first man. From God's hand this first man was made and he was like God. His name was Adam, which means "Mankind."

God brought all the different kinds of animals to Adam and told him they would be called whatever Adam wanted. So he called one a hippopotamus, and another a butterfly. He named the birds — everything from flamingo to pheasant.

When Adam had finished naming every single creature on earth, God saw that the animals were not able to be Adam's special friend.

So while Adam slept, God took a part of Adam and around that part he made someone who was like Adam, but different. She was the first woman. When Adam woke up he was very happy because now there was someone like him, someone who could be his friend and helper. But she did not have a name yet.

When God finished making Adam and the woman, he was pleased. He decided he would rest for one day, and bless all that he had made. That is why there is one day in every week that God has set aside for us to take a break from work and enjoy the good things he has given to each of us.

THE FIRST CHOICE
In the Image of God

Genesis 2.8-17, 25

God chose a special part of the earth and gave it to Adam and the woman. It was a garden called Eden. There flowers bloomed in the brightest colours and the sun shone warmly. In Eden all the animals lived peacefully with each other and no one was afraid.

Adam and the woman loved God very much, and they were thankful for the beautiful world he had given them.

They walked around their garden with no clothes on because they had no reason to feel embarrassed. For them there was one thing even better than all the dazzling flowers, tall trees, and lovely smells in Eden. They knew God cared for them and they had nothing to hide from him.

God told Adam and the woman they could do whatever they wanted. There was just one rule they must follow. God said, "You may eat fruit from any of the trees here except one. That is the tree of knowledge of good and evil." The two people understood.

All For a Piece of Fruit

Genesis 3.1-6

Of all the animals in Eden there was one craftier than the rest. That was the serpent. One day the serpent crept towards the woman and teased her. "Can you eat fruit from all the trees?" the serpent asked.

"Oh, yes," the woman answered. "We can eat fruit from every tree but one. God has warned Adam and me that if we eat fruit which comes from the tree in the middle of the garden we will die."

The serpent laughed at her. "You will not die! God just says you shouldn't eat from that tree because he does not want you to be like him and be able to tell good from bad."

After the serpent said this to her, the woman did not know what she should do. She walked over to the tall tree in the middle of the garden and looked up. The fruit did not look bad. She thought about disobeying God. She knew she had a choice to make. God had given her the freedom to choose whether to obey or disobey. So the woman chose. She chose to disobey God.

She picked a piece of fruit and took a bite. Then she brought the fruit to Adam and asked him to eat as well. When they had both taken a bite they suddenly knew that they had been bad to disobey God.

A Reason to Hide

Genesis 3.7-13

The very moment that Adam and the woman tasted the forbidden fruit, they saw things differently. They looked down at their bodies and realized that they had no clothes on. For the first time ever, they felt embarrassed. So they quickly started making clothes with which to cover themselves.

Suddenly they heard God moving through Eden in the cool evening breezes. They ran through their special garden, frantically looking for a place to hide.

The Lord God said to them, "Where are you?"

"Don't look, God. We are not wearing very much!" Adam called to God.

"Who told you you were naked? Have you eaten from the tree of knowledge of good and evil?" God asked.

Adam said, "The woman gave me some fruit to eat, so I did."

"But the serpent fooled me, and that's why I ate," the woman said.

No matter what they said, it felt as if a cloud were hanging over Adam and the woman. The sunshine felt cold and for the first time ever, the people were afraid.

Cut Off From God

Genesis 3.14–19

Adam and the woman were not sure what God might do. They had never disobeyed him before. Now all the bright happiness and security they had shared, in the garden which God had given them, seemed to be gone.

God said to the serpent, "Because you have tempted the woman to disobey me you must crawl on your belly in the dust. The woman and her children will always be your enemies."

Then God turned to Adam and the woman. The Lord was very sad because he must discipline his children now that they had done the wrong thing. God did this because he cared. He wanted Adam and the woman to know that every choice was their own, but that some choices led to good things while other choices could be painful.

To the woman God said, "Because you have disobeyed me I will make it very painful for you to give birth to children. But the special bond I have given you with Adam will remain, and you will be subject to him."

The Lord God looked at Adam. "Adam, because you have disobeyed me, whenever you try to grow plants so that you will have food to eat, it will be hard work for you. It will not come easily. And when you die, your body will go back to the dust, because that is where you came from."

Adam turned to the woman and took her hand.

Out of Eden

Genesis 3.20–24

Then God told them they must leave the garden of Eden, because they were not now allowed to eat from the tree of life.

Adam and the woman looked at each other. They were together, but they felt frightened of all that lay ahead. When they left Eden they

10

would have to work hard in order to find enough to eat.

Adam gave the woman a name then. He called her Eve, which means "Living."

Adam and Eve bowed their heads. They felt very sad. They knew God would continue to show his love for them. But the worst part of their punishment was that they would never

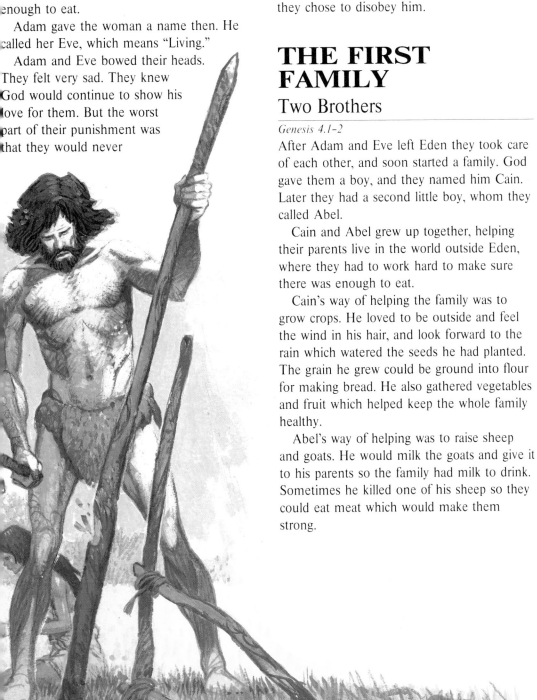

be as close to God as they had been before they chose to disobey him.

THE FIRST FAMILY
Two Brothers

Genesis 4.1-2

After Adam and Eve left Eden they took care of each other, and soon started a family. God gave them a boy, and they named him Cain. Later they had a second little boy, whom they called Abel.

Cain and Abel grew up together, helping their parents live in the world outside Eden, where they had to work hard to make sure there was enough to eat.

Cain's way of helping the family was to grow crops. He loved to be outside and feel the wind in his hair, and look forward to the rain which watered the seeds he had planted. The grain he grew could be ground into flour for making bread. He also gathered vegetables and fruit which helped keep the whole family healthy.

Abel's way of helping was to raise sheep and goats. He would milk the goats and give it to his parents so the family had milk to drink. Sometimes he killed one of his sheep so they could eat meat which would make them strong.

The Choice

Genesis 4.3-7

One day Cain gathered some of the crops he had grown and offered them to God as a present, a way of saying thank you for all God had done for the family. Abel did the same, but he chose the first lamb born to one of his sheep to give back to God.

God was pleased with Abel and his present, but he rejected Cain and his present.

This made Cain angry. God said to Cain, "Why are you angry? Why are you scowling? If you had done the right thing and chosen the best to give to me, you would be smiling because I would have been pleased with your gift. But you've done wrong. You have to learn to say 'no' to what is wrong, and choose to do good instead."

The First Murder

Genesis 4.8-16

Cain wanted to be angry. He did not think God was being fair. God had said Cain had a choice. Cain chose to be angry.

He came up with a plan. He called Abel out to the fields, where Cain had worked so hard to grow his crops. There, out in the open, Cain did something dreadful. He killed Abel.

God called to him, "Cain, where is your brother Abel?"

Cain pretended he did not know.

God said, "You have done wrong. As your punishment, you will no longer be able to grow your crops. I will not allow the land to give grain and fruit and vegetables to you. No matter how hard you work, the crops you grow will always die. Instead you must spend the rest of your life wandering, never finding a true home."

Cain had not thought of what might happen after he killed Abel. He was learning that every choice carries consequences. Now he regretted what he had done to his brother. After all, Abel had been Cain's best friend. He was also scared about where he would find food if he could not grow it.

Worst of all, although God promised to protect Cain from harm, Cain was going away from God's presence. God sent him to a land east of Eden, to the land of Nod, which means "Wandering."

A MAN NAMED NOAH
All the Pain

Genesis 4.17–6.12

In the years to come God gave many children to Adam and Eve, and to Cain and his wife. They too, had many children, who had children, who had children, just like your great-grandfather had your grandfather who had your father, who had you.

After some time, most of the people living on earth had chosen not to live close to God any more. They no longer taught their children to thank God for the good things he gave them. They chose to hurt and lie and do wrong, rather than be good.

God looked at the people and grew very sad. He saw that they no longer even tried to do right. He saw all the pain they caused each other and themselves, and he wished he had never created people with the rest of the animals on earth.

Unlike the animals, people did bad things just for the sake of hurting. God decided he would take away the lives on earth that he had created.

Noah Builds a Boat

Genesis 6.13-22

During this time, when so many people were bad, there was one man who was different. His name was Noah. Noah often asked God's help in living his life. Noah listened for God's answers and then obeyed him. This pleased God.

God told Noah, "I am going to put an end to all people. I will cause a huge flood to cover the land and everyone will drown. But I will spare you and those you love. Build a big boat, and build it in the way I tell you to. Then fill it with two of every type of animal. Fill it with food for yourselves and them. And you will be safe."

When Noah heard God's plans he grew afraid, yet he knew God could be trusted. So Noah did as God told him.

God gave Noah the plans for making the boat, which was called an ark. It was especially designed for floating, just right for surviving a flood.

As Noah built the ark, his neighbours did not know what to think. They said, "But where is the sea? We live near the desert."

Noah told them what God had said — that there was still time to say sorry to God and live good lives. But his neighbours just laughed.

THE GREAT FLOOD
The Voyage of the Ark

Genesis 7.1-16

When the ark was finished, Noah's family climbed in, and with them went the animals and birds, creeping creatures and crawling things. What a sight it was! And the noise was enough to bring Noah's neighbours out to watch and shake their heads all over again.

There were lions roaring, donkeys braying, dogs barking, birds singing, and sheep bleating. Two by two, the animals entered the ark, all different types and shapes and sizes. Tiny worms wiggled, horses pranced, and rabbits hopped.

When all the animals were inside, God closed the door to the boat. Then it began to rain.

The Rescue

Genesis 7.17–8.1

It rained and rained. The water poured out of the skies as if the clouds contained waterfalls, instead of raindrops.

For forty days and forty nights the rains fell. Noah's ark went higher and higher, carried by the water to heights as tall as mountains. In fact, the water rose so high, the mountains disappeared underwater.

As the land flooded, all the living things on earth drowned — all the people and animals and birds, for there were no dry places on which to live. The water was everywhere.

As days dragged into weeks, Noah and his family felt as though they had always been surrounded by the smells and sounds of a thousand animals. There was no difference between night and day, since they stayed inside all the time, and the sun could not shine anyway because dark rain clouds blocked its light.

God did not forget his promise to Noah. When the forty days were over, God sent a wind over the earth and the water level started to drop.

The End of the Storm

Genesis 8.2

Noah woke up to darkness, as he had since the storm started. But that morning something was different. He checked his family — they were still asleep. The animals were quiet. The ark rolled from one side to the other, as it had ever since the storm started. What was different?

Then he knew. Noah could hear the waves lapping the sides of the great boat. Before that day the sounds of rain had kept him from hearing the waves. The rains had finally stopped.

Noah ran through the boat, waking everyone up. "It's over! The flood is over! Oh, let's thank God for sparing us and ending the storm!" he shouted from one end of the boat to the other. So the family gathered to give their thanks and praise to God.

But it wasn't until months later that the waters went down enough for the ark to find a mountain-top on which to rest.

A Raven and a Dove

Genesis 8.3–14

Some months later, Noah and his family went on deck for the first time. All they could see was water in all directions, broken by the tip-tops of mountains poking their way above the surface.

Noah waited another month before he let a raven out to see if it could find dry land. But it was too early.

Then he let a dove fly away and try to find

a dry place to settle. At first the dove came back, but a week later Noah let the dove go again and this time it returned with an olive leaf in its mouth. That meant there were places dry enough for trees and plants to grow.

Noah waited one more week and then sent the dove out again, but this time it did not come back. The dove had found a place to land.

Many months after the storm had started, Noah took the roof off the ark and saw that water no longer covered the ground. Nearly two months later there was not even any mud left.

Noah and his family had been in the ark for a very long time and they were just as anxious as the animals to get out and start walking around again, exploring the fresh, clean earth.

A Promise In Every Rainbow

Genesis 8.15—9.17

God said to Noah, "You, your family, and all the animals may leave the boat, go on to the land, and build homes."

The animals could not wait to get off the ark. They tossed their heads and made even more noise leaving than they had when they got on. Shrieking and snorting, mooing and mewing, two by two they charged down the gangplank and made their way across the land

When the boat was empty, Noah and his family built a big table called an altar. There they thanked God for keeping them safe during the long time at sea.

When God heard their thanks, he was so pleased, he promised never to destroy all living creatures again. He promised that as long as the earth lasted, summer would follow winter, and day follow night.

Then God made something very special. Using every colour, he made the first rainbow "As a sign of my promise never to flood the whole earth again, I have set my rainbow in the clouds."

THE TOWER OF BABEL

The City Builders

Genesis 10.1–11.4

Noah's sons had many children who had many children, who had many more children. The families spread out across the land, learning how to farm, raise animals, and build great cities.

Because they all came from the same family, all the people spoke the same language. When strangers came from far away, anyone could understand them when they spoke.

Some of the people said, "Let's build the biggest and best city ever built so we can be famous and not have to wander any more. We will finally have a home."

The people were clever. Instead of using stones they made bricks, and stuck the bricks together with tar, instead of mortar. Their walls were the strongest and highest ever. And they were very proud of themselves, choosing not to thank God for the materials they used for building.

"We are so clever," they said.

Higher Than the Clouds

Genesis 11.5-9

Inside the city was a huge tower. The people thought they were such good builders, they could make that tower as high as the sky.

When God saw what the people were trying to do, he knew he must stop them or they would soon think of themselves as gods, instead of people. They would be too proud. So he mixed up their language.

The people no longer spoke one language but many. If one man said "Hello," the other man did not know what he had said.

He thought he might be saying, "Could I borrow your tools?" It was hard to get anything done, let alone finish a great tower.

The city they never finished building was called Babel, which means "Mixed Up," because there the Lord mixed up the language of the whole world.

Then God caused the people to scatter to many different parts of the earth, so now there were people living everywhere, and there was no way at all for them to plot and scheme and grow proud of themselves.

ABRAM THE WANDERER
God Chooses Abram

Genesis 12.1-3

Many years later there lived a man named Abram. He and his wife Sarai lived in the land of Haran. They had many sheep, cattle, goats, and camels. Abram and Sarai were happy.

Although Abram and Sarai stored their things in tents, they often slept outside. Night time in the desert helped to bring God very close. They could feel his presence when the sky stretched like an endless blanket of stars. Often on such nights, Abram and Sarai wished for a child. But the years went by and none came.

One star-filled desert night, when the creatures of the dark were singing and Sarai lay asleep at his side, Abram heard God speaking to him.

Abram walked a short way into the desert. There God told Abram some amazing things. "Abram, I will make you into a great nation and I will take care of you. And all people everywhere will be blessed because of you."

A Move In the Right Direction

Genesis 12.4-9

Abram lay shaking in the sand. He could not believe his ears. Why had God chosen him?

The Lord told Abram to leave his home at Haran. Even though Abram did not know where the Lord would lead him and his family, he obeyed God. He trusted that God would take care of him.

He told Sarai what had happened and she trusted, too. She ordered everyone to pack the tents onto the camels. "Gather the food into bundles and get ready for a long trip," she told them.

"But where are we going?" they asked.

"I do not know," she said, smiling. Both Abram and Sarai were happy to wait for God to tell them where they were going.

God led Abram and Sarai, all the camels, hundreds of sheep and goats, many servants and all their children to the land of Canaan. There the Lord said to Abram, "This is the land I will give to your children." But God did not want Abram to stop in Canaan. Not yet.

SARAI AND ABRAM

A Close Call With Pharaoh

Genesis 12.10–16

Sarai and Abram followed wherever God led them through the desert. But there came a time when they ran out of food. So they went to Egypt where they had heard there was enough to eat.

Just before they arrived Abram said, "Sarai, tell the Egyptians you are my sister. I am afraid the king of Egypt might try to kill me so he can marry you."

He was right. When Abram and Sarai and all their animals and servants arrived in Egypt, the king, or Pharaoh, heard of Sarai's beauty and wanted to marry her. He sent his soldiers to bring her back to the palace.

When Sarai was at the Egyptian palace, Pharaoh sent many donkeys, cattle, servants and camels to Abram in thanks for his sister. But of course, Sarai was not his sister, and Abram felt miserable.

Together Again

Genesis 12.17–20

Because Pharaoh had taken Sarai, the Lord made him and his household ill with many different diseases. Pharaoh realized he must have offended God when Sarai came into his palace. He realized Sarai must be Abram's wife, not sister, and that God was punishing him for trying to marry her when she already had a husband.

Pharaoh sent for Abram, "Why did you do this to me? Why did you lie and say Sarai was your sister? You have caused nothing but trouble for me. Here," Pharaoh shouted, "take her back and get out of Egypt!"

Abram gave Sarai a big hug. They were both very happy to be back together. They packed all their belongings, including the food they had come for, and headed out of Egypt.

The Promise of God

Genesis 13.14–18

Abram and Sarai travelled back to the land of
Canaan. There the Lord said, "Abram, take a
good look. One day I will give this land to you
and your children. I will make your family
very large. They will become as many as the
grains of dust on the ground, too many to
count."

Once again, Abram was amazed at all God promised him. He told Sarai and she believed, too. They still had had no children, but they trusted God and were willing to wait.

Abram and Sarai moved their tents near the sacred trees of Mamre at Hebron. The big trees there gave them plenty of shade. Many years passed and there was still one thing they wished for, and that was a child. So many years had gone by, though, that Sarai was too old to have children. Abram and Sarai did not understand how God could have promised them children. They felt confused. What had God meant?

Where Are the Children?

Genesis 15.1–21

Then, one night, Abram heard God speak to him again.

Abram, who was by then an old man, said, "Lord, the one thing you could give me you have not, and that is a child. Why haven't we had any children?"

"You will have a child, though, Abram," God said. "Look up and count the stars."

Abram saw the sky stretch from horizon to horizon, stars blinking in every direction, and

your side helps you along step by step. That's what God did for Abram. He stayed by his side, every step of his life.

New Names For a Special People

Genesis 17.1-27

Abram waited, and believed that God would keep his word. The years went by until, finally, Abram was ninety-nine years old. Then the Lord appeared to Abram again and reminded him of the promise he had made.

As a sign of how serious the promise was, God asked Abram to make a special mark on his body and see that all the men and boys in his camp did the same. This showed the promise was meant to last for ever. God would not forget.

Then he gave Abram and Sarai new names. Abram became Abraham, which means "Father of Many." And Sarai became Sarah, which means "Princess."

God promised Abraham that Sarah would have a baby and that the baby would grow into the father of many children. They would all become God's chosen people.

he wondered what God could mean.

"One day there will be as many children of your children as there are stars," God said.

Abram had a choice. He could decide not to believe the Lord because he did not understand how God could do this great thing. Or Abram could choose to trust what God said, even though he had no idea how it would happen.

It was a little like letting someone else lead you through a room when your eyes are closed. You cannot see, but the person by

Three Visitors Catch Sarah By Surprise

Genesis 18.1-15

A short time later, Abraham saw three men walking nearby. He ran over to them and bowed low. "Please, come and stay with us, and let me get you something to eat and drink."

Abraham told Sarah to bake some bread as fast as she could. Then he hurried to kill his fattest, choicest calf and told his servant to cook it as quickly, but as well, as he could.

Now Abraham did not realize that one of the three visitors was actually the Lord. When Abraham gave the visitors their food, the Lord said, "Where is your wife Sarah?"

"In the tent," Abraham said.

"Sarah will soon have a son," the Lord said.

Sarah had been listening through the tent wall. When she heard this, she thought it a strange joke by the visitor. They were too old for babies. So she laughed.

Then the visitor said, "Why did Sarah laugh? Is anything too hard for the Lord to do?" And when he said that, Abraham knew the visitor was the Lord.

TWO CITIES BECOME DUST
On the Way to Sodom

Genesis 18.16-33

When it was time for the men to leave, Abraham walked with them to the top of a nearby hill. From there they looked down on the city of Sodom.

The Lord said, "I have heard how terribly evil the people are who live in Sodom. If it is true, then I will destroy that place."

Then the two men who had travelled with the Lord, who were really angels in disguise, set off for Sodom. The Lord stayed with Abraham.

Abraham was not sure what he should do. There was a question he wanted to ask of the Lord, but did he dare? He knew though, that the Lord was his friend as well as his God. So he swallowed hard and asked, "Lord, what if there are fifty good people in Sodom? What will happen to them? It would not be like you to kill the good people with the bad."

The Lord said, "I will not harm the city if there are fifty people who still care."

Then Abraham repeated his question several times, each time using smaller numbers. Would he spare the city for forty-five good people, for forty, thirty, twenty, or for ten? Each time the Lord replied that he would spare the city if there were that number of good people.

Lot Is Rescued

Genesis 19.1-29

The only bright spot in the evil city of Sodom was a man called Lot. Lot was a nephew of Abraham. He lived in Sodom with his wife and two daughters. Lot met the angels, who were disguised as men, and said, "Come to my house. There you will be safe from the people here."

It was dark, and Lot and his guests had

SONS OF DIFFERENT MOTHERS

Abraham's First Son — His Mother Was a Slave

Genesis 16.1–15; 21.9–21; 25.12–18

Sarah decided she would not wait until God finally gave her a child. So she told her slave girl, Hagar, that she and Abraham could have a baby. When Hagar knew she was pregnant, she teased Sarah, who had no children. So Sarah was cruel to Hagar.

The Lord comforted Hagar. "One day the sons of your son, Ishmael, will be too many to count. I will watch over them and take care of them."

But bad became worse. When Sarah finally had a baby of her own, she sent Hagar and her son into the desert.

Hagar did not have much food and water. They walked and walked, over the dunes, through the hot desert. There was no place to rest in the shade, there were no trees, no

finished eating, when suddenly, they heard shouting outside. Lot opened the door and saw hundreds of men carrying torches and shoving their way towards his home. "Give us the two men who are visiting you," they shouted at Lot.

Then the angels caused all the evil men outside to go blind. That way they could not even find the door to Lot's house. "Hurry," the angels said to Lot. "The Lord cannot stand the evil of Sodom and he will destroy it by tomorrow." The angels led Lot, his two daughters, and his wife out of the city in a great hurry.

Then, just after sunrise, the Lord caused fire to come out of the sky and drop on to Sodom and nearby Gomorrah, which was also an evil place. Lot's wife was not supposed to, but she looked back to watch. Instantly she became a pillar of salt.

God had kept his promise to Abraham. He took care of the good people in Sodom.

lants, just sand stretching for mile after mile. Mother and son began to cry.

Then God opened Hagar's eyes and she saw a well of water. From then on God made sure Hagar and Ishmael always had enough to eat and drink.

As Ishmael grew older, he became an expert with the bow and arrow. God kept his promise and the many sons of Ishmael became a nation apart from the one God promised to Abraham.

saac Is Born

Genesis 21.1–8

God had promised Sarah and Abraham a child, and Sarah should not have worried. When the three strangers visited Sarah and Abraham, the Lord promised they would have a baby within a year.

Sure enough, in less than a year the impossible happened. Sarah, far too old to have children, gave birth to a son. Abraham was one hundred years old when Sarah's baby was born. He and Sarah were so happy and thankful to God for finally answering their prayers.

The child made them so happy, they would often laugh together. So they called the baby Isaac, which means "He Laughs." The boy was a good reason to laugh and be happy.

THE HARDEST TEST OF ALL
Abraham and Isaac

Genesis 22.1–2

"Abraham!" the voice of God called. "Take your son, your special son Isaac. I know how

much you love him, and this is why I ask you to do this difficult thing. I want you to give Isaac back to me." This meant Isaac would have to die.

Abraham said nothing. The God he knew would never want Abraham to kill his own son. He knew that. God had promised that Isaac would have many children. How could that happen if Isaac were dead?

Abraham knew he could choose not to trust God, say "no," run in fear, and try and hide. But who can hide from God?

Or he could choose to trust. Perhaps there was more to God's plan than first seemed to be there.

True Trust

Genesis 22.3-8

Early the next morning Abraham got up and woke Isaac. "Come, Isaac, we are going on a journey." Isaac was excited. He liked nothing better than to go travelling with his father.

Abraham asked Isaac to carry the wood for the sacrifice they were going to make to God, while he carried the knife. Isaac had often worshipped the Lord with his father. He knew how important it was to give thanks to God for all the good things God gave them. But this time his father was quieter than usual. And besides, there was something missing.

"Father?" Isaac asked.

"Yes, my son," Abraham replied.

"The fire and wood are here," Isaac said, "but where is the lamb which we usually offer?"

Abraham answered, "God will provide one."

Saved In Time

Genesis 22.9-19

After three days of travel, they reached their destination. Abraham told Isaac to climb on to the altar.

Isaac did not know what his father intended to do.

Abraham stood over Isaac, holding the knife up high. He was just about to kill his son when an angel called to him from heaven, "Abraham, Abraham!" Abraham stopped, his hand in mid-air. "Don't hurt the boy. Your willingness to do what God asked shows that you trust God with everything, even the life of your special son, Isaac."

Abraham looked and saw a ram whose horns were caught in a nearby bush. That was the offering God had provided.

Isaac was still trembling as his father helped him from the altar.

The angel called down from heaven again.
"Abraham, God says that because you trusted
him completely, he will make your family as
many as the stars in the sky. All the other
nations in the world will be blessed through
you."

Adventure Story Bible Old Testament

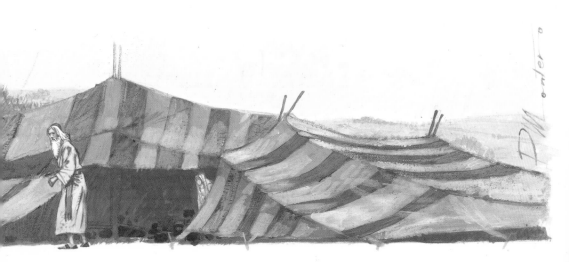

New Testament